Blessings,
Helen Walters

Growing Under the Shadow of His Wings

Life Lessons with Psalms

by
Helen Walters

"But I still my soul and make it quiet,
like a child upon its mother's breast;
my soul is quieted within me."
Psalm 131:3

A deeply personal and introspective twelve-lesson
study guide for spiritual growth with the Psalms,
taken from The Psalter, The Book of Common Prayer.

authorHOUSE

1663 Liberty Drive, Suite 200
Bloomington, Indiana 47403
(800) 839-8640
www.AuthorHouse.com

© 2004 Helen Walters
All Rights Reserved.

No part of this book may be reproduced, stored in a retrieval system, or transmitted by any means without the written permission of the author.

First published by AuthorHouse 10/07/04

ISBN: 1-4184-9260-4 (e)
ISBN: 1-4184-9259-0 (sc)

Library of Congress Control Number: 2004098055

Printed in the United States of America
Bloomington, Indiana

This book is printed on acid-free paper.

Cover artwork by Mark Walters (the author's son), owner of Hot Fish Studios.

Under the loving shadow
Of your wings O God,
Will I take refuge,
Will I rejoice!

My joy and trust
I place in you O Lord,
In hope for the
Desires of my heart.
-HPW

After: Psalm 17:8
Psalm 36:7
Psalm 57:1
Psalm 63:7
Psalm 91:4

The Book of Psalms

When the idea for this book came into my head, I had just finished reading from the Psalter. It struck me that because they are so beloved, the psalms would be the perfect accompaniment for my lessons.

The book of Psalms is a body of liturgical poetry, hymns, and personal devotions. While widely attributed to David, it is also believed that there were possibly other authors such as Moses, Solomon, Asaph, Ethan, and the sons of Korah. Some of the last psalms are anonymous.

Regardless of who wrote what, the psalms are an ancient and beautiful testimony to the love of God for his children.

-HPW

Preface/Dedication

In the hectic pace of life in the 21ST century, there is such peace, such joy in simply opening the book of Psalms. I never cease to be amazed at the beauty of the words and the relevance (even today) of their meaning.

This book was written to encourage and strengthen spiritual growth and to attempt to let that growth permeate every moment of every life.

God is so incredibly caring and kind, patient and tolerant. I feel called to invite you, the reader, to accompany me as we journey together toward a closer relationship with this Loving Creator.

I would especially like to express my thanks to my late mother, Helen Chambers Price, to my sons, Joel Walters and Mark Walters, and a number of dear friends and mentors, among them Fran Cash, Dr. Jeannie Flinn, Jeanette Gannon, Carol Harwood, The Rev. Michael Mills, Linda Milton, Edward Morris, The Rev. Frederick Philputt, Pat Pollino, Charlotte Rundell, The Rev. Larry Smith, and

Lynne Wachter, who have never stopped believing in me and loving me. They have my love and humble appreciation in return.

-HPW

July 2001

And I thank our God for all the many blessings of my life, but especially for the existence of the Episcopal Church of the Incarnation in Dallas, Texas, where I was taken as a very young child in 1944. There, with my maternal grandmother, Elizabeth Bengel Chambers, and mother, Helen Chambers Price, and my aunt, Gertrude Chambers Shull, I was given a wonderful foundation on which to build my soul growth. Now, today, some fifty-six years later, I still call Incarnation home and am still in spiritual growth there.

Introduction

Welcome to Growing Under the Shadow of His Wings!

I love the psalms, and I love God. I am not a theologian; there is no way I would ever pretend to be a Biblical scholar. I am simply an ordinary person like each of you, possessing strengths and weaknesses, having experienced joy and tragedy, and still very much growing on my faith journey.

Life is complicated and stressful. We have so many outside influences, so many choices and frustrations. I designed this book for self-help through the spiritual support of the book of Psalms.

To benefit from the book and/or class, you must be willing to be honest with yourself. Anything shared in a class setting should remain within the class so that everyone feels comfortable. Your workbook has spaces for your answers; I hope that you will write freely in order to document your own journey's experiences. And I hope too that by doing so, Growing Under the Shadow of His Wings will become a personal journal of spiritual growth.

Blessings to each of you,

-HPW

Growing under the shadow of God's wings is taken from Psalm 57:1

Table of Contents

Chapter I – Self 1

Chapter II – Forgiveness 11

Chapter III – Acceptance 21

Chapter IV – Growth and Values 29

Chapter V – Friendship 37

Chapter VI – Prayer Life / Methods of Prayer 43

Chapter VII – Boundaries and Priorities / Choices 53

Chapter VIII – Giving 63

Chapter IX – Joy, Anger, and Grief 69

Chapter X – Praise 79

Chapter XI – The Words of God 85

Chapter XII – Sharing God With Others 91

Prayer of Affirmation

Dear God,

You are worthy of praise and reverence.

You made me.

I acknowledge your love for me, and I humbly give you thanks.

I acknowledge that I am a person of worth, and I implore your kind compassion and generous spirit to guide me as I journey closer to you with your blessed son Jesus as my constant companion.

Amen

Chapter I – Self
Who Are You Really, and
Where Did You Come From?

*"Your hands have made me
and fashioned me; give me understanding,
that I may learn your commandments."* Psalm 119:73

You are a child of God, no ifs, ands, or buts. No matter what you might think or how you might feel, You Are A Child of God. <u>His</u> hands have made <u>you</u>.

We are all unique. A complex combination of genes plus a variety of childhood environments contributes to who we are and where we came from. Throughout our lives, we have many choices. We can lay blame for faults and failures on our childhood, our parents, our economic situation. We can wallow in self-pity and become negative– minded and unpleasant to be around. Or we can give thanks for our blessings and try to make the best of who we are and what we have.

Some of us are fortunate to have been reared in loving, nurturing homes. Others have had to overcome abusive homes - homes where there was emotional, verbal, or physical abuse. It is a sad fact that the latter exists, but it is a real challenge and a testimony of faith and belief to overcome these circumstances.

> "For God alone my soul in silence waits; from him comes my salvation."
> -Psalm 62:1

There are various methods for dealing with our past lives: counseling, support groups, escapism through work, alcohol, sex, drugs and so on. But in the final analysis, there are three proven ways to overcome any past negativity.

First, we must seek God's help. We must openly and honestly give our burden to him.

This does not mean telling God how we hurt and then continuing to drag the sorrows around like millstones around our necks. We do not really show trust in God if we give him our cares and then snatch them back.

> "To you, O Lord, I lift up my soul;
> my God, I put my trust in you; let me
> not be humiliated, nor let my enemies
> triumph over me." Psalm 25

Self

Secondly, we must forgive anyone and anything that has hurt us in the past. This is often difficult, but only in doing so can we be free of the thoughts and remembrances that stifle us. When we cling to the pain inflicted by others, we allow them to retain control and thereby imprison our very souls.

"For you, O Lord, are good and forgiving,
And great is your love toward all who call upon you." Psalm 86:5

Third, we need to reach out. By giving to others and by seeking the best for them, we take our focus off ourselves and give ourselves opportunity for growth. When we pray for others, when we give to and share with others, we open up more room for God to enter in and our hurts to fade away.

Growing Under the Shadow of His Wings

"I have become a portent to many;
but you are my refuge and my strength." Psalm 71:7

Who are you? Describe yourself.

What are your best characteristics? Your worst (if any!)?

Where did you come from? Describe your childhood, the good and the bad.

Self

What is your favorite memory?

The least favorite memory? Describe it and then GIVE IT TO GOD!

Growing Under the Shadow of His Wings

Read Psalms 69, 70 and 71.

What are your feelings afterward?

Psalm 69:

Psalm 70:

Psalm 71:

Self

Years ago, I discovered Joni Eareckson Tada. As a young woman, she was left paralyzed as the result of a diving accident. Her struggles were many, but she emerged as a beautiful and talented writer, singer, and artist. When I am tempted to wallow in self-pity, I think of the beautiful giving spirit of Joni, and I realize that I have much to be thankful for. And I give God great thanks for the joy that Joni's many talents bring.

List those people you know that you are thankful for:	Relationship (family member, friend, co-worker, etc.)	The reason I appreciate this person:

The person I am most thankful for was my mother. She was gentle, kind, generous, gracious, soft-spoken, mild-mannered, and very patient. She was many things that I am not. I believe I possess many good qualities, thoughtfulness and cheerfulness among them. But I am not particularly quiet or patient! I have always thought that anything good that I am I owe to God, of course, and to my precious and beautiful mother. She instilled in me the feelings of confidence and worth, and also the desire to be all I could be. I shall be forever grateful to God for her presence in my life. Her love and guidance have been among my greatest blessings.

Self

How's Your Ego?

You may be the president of a large corporation or you may be a school janitor, but how's your ego? Inflated like a hot air balloon (balloons pop, you know) or crawling along the floor?

In God's sight, we are all his children. He made each of us. Granted, he bestowed different gifts and abilities, but we all have a place in this world. And we are all able to give back to him through praise, prayer, love for him and love for others.

> "He counts the number of the stars
> And calls them all by their names." –Psalm 147:4

If God is this mindful of stars, how much more mindful is he of us!

Read Psalm 147 and record your thoughts:

Growing Under the Shadow of His Wings

Psalm 71 portrays growing old with God. Read this psalm and record your thoughts:

"In thee, O Lord, do I
take refuge; let me never
be put to shame!" – Psalm 71:1

Chapter II – Forgiveness

"When my mind became embittered,
I was sorely wounded in my heart." Psalm 73:21

Some are called to bear more hurt than others. It is really not for us to understand completely. We do not have the capacity to fathom many of life's tragedies. Did your parents treat you unfairly? Have you had one or more failed marriages? Does career success elude you? Is your health poor? <u>No one has a perfect life!</u> We frequently think the grass looks greener on the other side of the fence, but if we go there, we find a few weeds as well. Also, some people hurt us because they want to be Number One – jealousy and envy occur. We must pray for them.

Growing Under the Shadow of His Wings

Read Psalms 102 and 103.

Contrast the despair of Psalm 102 (verses 1-11) with the hopeful praise of Psalm 103.

How do you relate to Psalm 102?

Psalm 103? (esp. verses 8, 10, 13)

Forgiveness

Some people flippantly admonish "Deal the hand you were dealt", or "When life gives you lemons, make lemonade." Both sound easy and trite, but we can not overcome cruel treatment, unfortunate circumstances, hatred, and unfairness of any kind <u>unless</u> we seek (and cling to) God.

"Fight those who fight me, O Lord;
attack those who are attacking me.
Take up shield and armor and rise
up to help me." Psalm 35:1,2

"There is great solace and beauty in Psalm 62, particularly verse 1 and verses 6 and 7.

"For God alone my soul in silence waits;
from him comes my salvation."
and
"For God alone my soul in silence waits; truly, my hope is in him.
He alone is my rock and my salvation, my stronghold, so that I
shall not be shaken."

There are those who say, "I might forgive, but I can never forget." This way of thinking is not true and complete forgiveness. It allows the perpetrator to maintain a hold over the one who has been hurt or mistreated. It allows the perpetrator to keep control of a part of the soul. It is difficult to forgive someone who has stolen,

Growing Under the Shadow of His Wings

slandered, betrayed, raped, or killed, but the judgement is for God's hands. When I am tempted to be judgmental or condescending, I think about the verse in Psalm 9:16 that says, "The Lord is known by his acts of justice; the wicked are trapped in the works of their own hands.", and I pull up short. I need forgiveness, too. And I need to remember Psalm 86:5 "For you, O Lord, are good and forgiving, and great is your love toward all who call upon you."

Are there any areas, issues, or persons in your life of unresolved forgiving? Write a brief synopsis here, and then write your own prayer asking God for help. Resolve to say <u>your</u> prayer daily. <u>And resolve to forgive</u>. It is very hard sometimes to do this, but it is also very freeing. Say <u>your</u> prayer of forgiveness daily and feel the release!

Forgiveness

In striving to forgive others, we sometimes forget to forgive ourselves. No one is perfect. We all do things, say things, or think things we shouldn't. Sometimes things happen totally beyond our control at the moment, and we assume guilt and blame ourselves over and over again.

For years, I blamed myself for a failed marriage. The man I married was my college sweetheart, and I thought we were the ideal romantic and glamorous couple. I also knew he liked to drink beer and mixed drinks, but how could I have foreseen that he would become physically abusive? Being hit, slapped, and choked for no reason at all was not my fault. I divorced him, but it took many years before I could forgive myself for this poor choice in a mate. Some situations are tragic beyond all comprehension. We cannot second-guess life. Accidents and illnesses happen. When a loved one is killed in an auto accident or dies suddenly, we must turn to God. A precious mother found her only two children inside a freezer where they had gone during a game of hide and seek. Of course, she was not at fault. But imagine her grief; her despair is beyond comprehension. It brings to mind Psalm 69:4: "I have grown weary with my crying." Victims of shootings, natural disasters, suicides, and other horrific situations leave behind loved ones asking why, harboring unwarranted guilt and frustration. It is only through our love for God that we can get through these situations. God loves us very much. He forgives us, and we must learn to forgive ourselves. Psalm 70:1 begs, "Be pleased, O God, to deliver me, O Lord, make haste to help me."

Growing Under the Shadow of His Wings

What situations in your life do you feel you need to forgive yourself for?

Forgiveness

Holy Father, for any unkind thought, word, or deed I may have had, said, or done, I humbly beg your forgiveness. Accept my appreciation for your love and blessings. Fill me with your Holy Spirit and guide me on the path you would have me take. I praise you for your loving compassion. Amen.

-HPW

Write your own prayer here:

Some people hurt us because they want to be Number One. Jealousy and envy rear their heads. We must continue to pray for them.

Stop "beating yourself up"!

We cannot always live without sin, BUT we can live in the knowledge that we can be forgiven.

God loves us. He does not deserve our mistrust when we do not accept his forgiveness, or when we do not forgive others, and he does not want us drowning in guilt.

Jesus suffered and died on the cross for our sins.

His death atones for anything we have done or may do.

However, we must confess, we must ask for this forgiveness, and we must try to change for the better. And we must forgive ourselves and others.

God's grace surrounds us.

Try this –

Visualize the cross of Jesus.
Now place your hurts, cares, and anger there.
Do not waste God's precious gift to us!
Leave your hurts, cares, and anger at the foot of the cross.
Find freedom in the love of God.
Take the hand of Jesus and go forth in joy.

Message to a Child of God

You are loved.

You are forgiven.

You are trusted.

Go and sin no more.

We will not speak of this again.

We should not continue to chastise ourselves once we ask for forgiveness. God knows our weaknesses and our frailties – and he is compassionate. It does us no good to keep harping on the same guilt, the same sin. "Beating a dead horse" is not being willing to accept the forgiveness of our loving God. We make the death of Jesus on the cross into nothingness when we do not accept the gift that it represents. We need to show our love for God and move on with our lives.

Chapter III – Acceptance

"What is man (or woman) that you
should be mindful of him (or her)?" Psalm 8:15

Psalm 8 goes on to say that God has made us only a little lower than the angels, that we are adorned with glory and honor. Wow! We can not ask for more, yet we often treat ourselves and one another in very inferior ways.

What is acceptance anyway? The dictionary defines it as being accepted or believed; unconditional reception. If God has made us only a little lower than the angels, how can we treat ourselves and others as lesser beings? When we fail to listen, to be compassionate or caring, we are failing in acceptance. Here I am not referring to unacceptable behavior like vulgarity or uncleaness, but rather individual differences. Each of us has a unique and special personality. I may love chocolate meringue pie and hate rhubarb pie. I may like to pass the peace in church or I may not. This does not mean that there is anything wrong with rhubarb pie, or with passing the peace or not passing the peace. It simply means that we are individuals with very different likes and dislikes.

Think of someone that you consider very different, maybe even a little "strange."

Jot down your thoughts about this person and what makes him/her unacceptable to you:

Now list things you do find pleasing or acceptable about this person:

Acceptance

Are they still as unacceptable as you first thought? How would you explain your feelings to God?

God made each of us. When we reject another individual, we are in a sense rejecting God. A person may be tall, short, skinny, fat, gay, lesbian, shy, vivacious, upstanding, or criminal. God made each of us. We must pray for tolerance and compassion, for acceptance of others as fellow children of God.

"Steadfast love is yours, O Lord,
for you repay everyone
according to his (or her) deeds." Psalm 62:14

Growing Under the Shadow of His Wings

      We cannot possibly know all the deeds, actions, and thoughts of another human being. I taught school for many years, and occasionally someone would inquire about another teacher's ability. My stock answer was, " I don't know – I'm too busy teaching in my own classroom." There were times when I sensed a certain teacher might be lax or negligent, but I had to remind myself that I didn't (and couldn't) really know about someone else if I was busy teaching my own students.

Read Psalm 139. God created our inmost parts (verse 12) and knows our every thought (verse 1). If God knows all and sees all and still loves us, how can we not accept one another?

Jot down your thoughts after reading this psalm.

Acceptance

Acceptance is often based on modes of dress, levels of education, socio-economic status, physical attractiveness, and so forth. But true acceptance needs to be based on our love of God. Jesus said, "Love one another as I have loved you." John 13:34

Have you ever felt unaccepted?

If so, why, when, and where?

How did you respond?

Do you find anyone in particular unacceptable?

If so, who, why, when, and where?

How could you change your feelings as a child of God?

Acceptance

Psalm 69:35 advises: "For the Lord listens to the needy, and his prisoners he does not despise." With God, there is compassion and loving tolerance for all. <u>There is acceptance.</u> And Psalm 62:14 teaches: "Steadfast love is yours, O Lord, for you repay everyone according to his deeds." Even in God's judgement, there is still acceptance for the soul. Psalm 116:10 admonishes, "How shall I repay the Lord for all the good things he has done for me?"

Acceptance is a two-way street. We must accept the love of God and his teachings. We must accept the uniqueness of his children and of ourselves as being his creations; created in love.

What can I do to show my acceptance of God and his word; of God and those he has created?

Chapter IV – Growth and Values

"Teach me, O Lord, the way of your
statutes and I shall keep it to the end." Psalm 119:33

If we stop seeking God, we might as well be dead. There is no joy on earth comparable to the relationship we are all able to have with our loving and caring Heavenly Father. Growth involves stretching, thirsting, seeking, falling, and getting back up, then falling again, but always getting back up. We may crawl, walk, or run toward God, but our growth will involve pain and discipline. It requires us to give, and it requires us to trust. It requires self-control.

Throughout my many years of teaching, I occasionally lost my temper and blurted out a response before I really thought about it. The response might have been to a student, parent, or co-worker. We are all guilty of speaking abruptly or rudely – perhaps to a friend or a spouse. In my classroom, I had a poster hanging on which I had printed Thumper's words from Walt Disney's famous and beloved movie classic, Bambi. "If you can't say something nice, don't say nothin' at all." It is hard, but we would all do well to remember this admonition.

Can you think of a time/times when you spoke abruptly and later regretted it? Write your thoughts here:

Psalm 39:1 guides us: "I will keep watch upon my ways so that I do not offend with my tongue."

Bible study with church friends or simply reading the Bible at home leads us to a closer walk with God. Working with a spiritual adviser gives us opportunities to stretch and grow through open discussion.

What are you doing or what would you like to do for personal growth?

Growth and Values

"Give me understanding, and I shall keep your law;
I shall keep it with all my heart." Psalm 119:34

How can we give and grow toward God? When we give of ourselves, our time and talents, we show acceptance of and love for God's children other than ourselves. Giving need not be expensive. It can be cards or phone calls to shut-ins. It could be reading a book to a class and giving the over-worked teacher a break. It could be delivering meals to the lonely elderly and spending a few minutes in conversation. It could be a bouquet of fresh flowers for no reason at all other than love for a special friend. When we show kindness and generosity of spirit, we demonstrate to God that we cherish his creations. In giving to others, we ultimately give to ourselves.

Can you think of some tangible ways to show God you are growing toward him?

True growth comes from defining our values. We need to know what is important to us before we can continue to grow. Values mold and shape our behavior and determine our goals.

What do you value most?

How are your values reflected in your daily life?

Growth and Values

> "Happy are they who observe his decrees and seek him with all their hearts. Who never do any wrong, but always walk in his ways. You laid down your commandments, that we should fully keep them. Oh, that my ways were made direct that I might keep your statutes! Then I should not be put to shame, when I regard all your commandments." Psalm 119:2-6

In the book of II Peter Chapter 3, verse 18, we are charged to "grow in grace and knowledge of our Lord and savior Jesus Christ."

A beautiful form of growth is prayer – prayer to God for others, for ourselves, for appreciation of his goodness. Prayer is an example of our self-discipline to spend time with God. We need to praise as well as petition.

Write your most recent prayer requests here:

Were they answered, and if so, how?

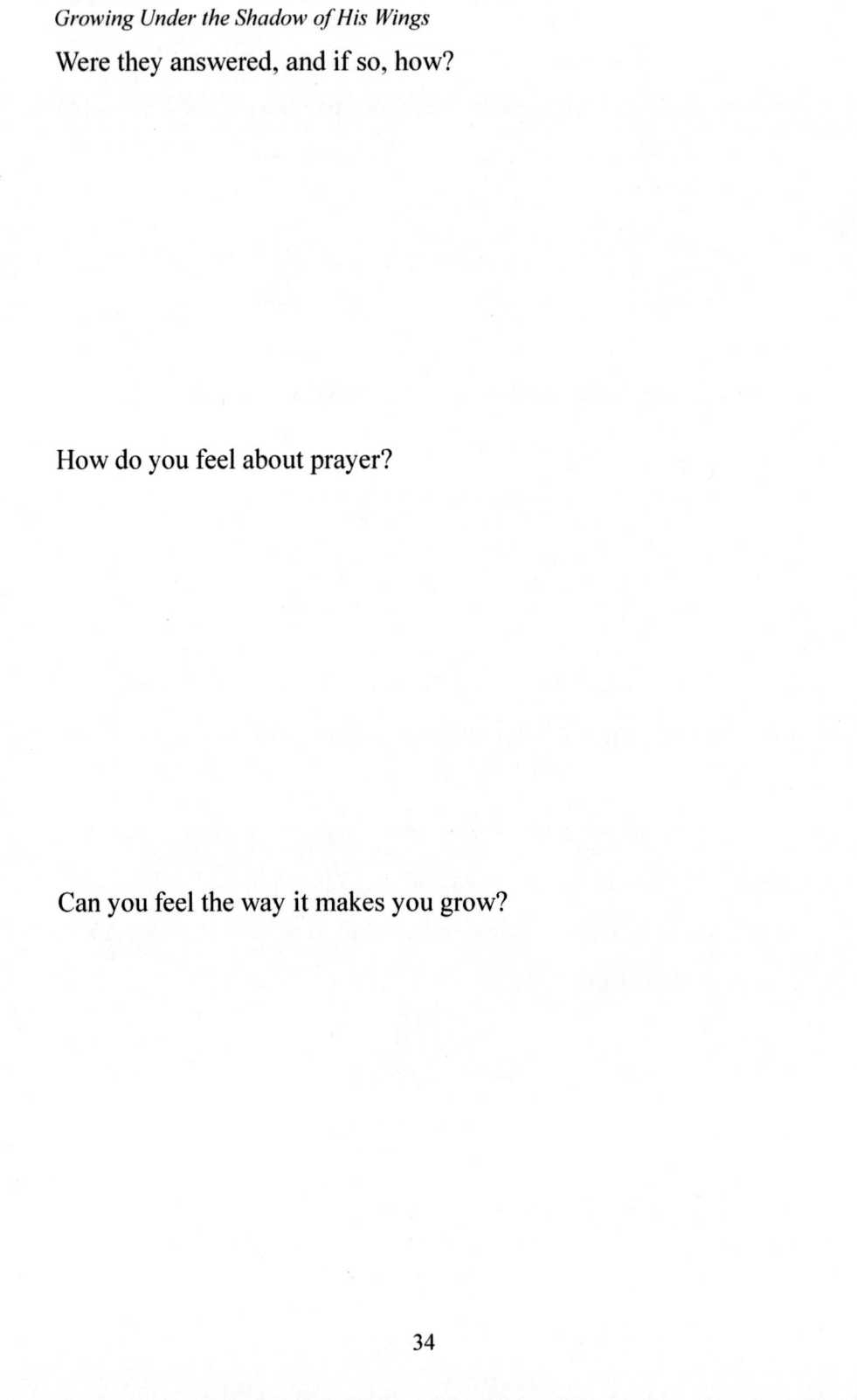

How do you feel about prayer?

Can you feel the way it makes you grow?

Growth and Values

Write your own prayer here. Tell God of your desire to grow closer to him, ask him to help you, and don't forget to thank him.

We rush from place to place, thing to thing, person to person. We need to remember that God is already there!

Chapter V – Friendship

"We are like a puff of wind;
our days are like a passing shadow." Psalm 144:4

As we journey through life, friends are a blessing of nurturing and comfort – a true gift from God. But friends require care. They require respect, and they require nurturing and comfort in return. It's that old two-way street again! Being a true friend requires patience, tolerance, and an understanding of each other's unique differences. It also requires forgiveness. For more than thirty years, I have maintained friendships with several different people. These friendships have been built on trust, honesty, and kindness. We have a shared history with one another. We may not talk or write for many months, but like a comfortable old pair of house shoes, we can always pick up where we left off. We still "fit." And so it is with God. The shared history, the trust, and the kindness are ours for the taking. All we have to do is be willing to accept it and give trust and kindness in return.

Growing Under the Shadow of His Wings

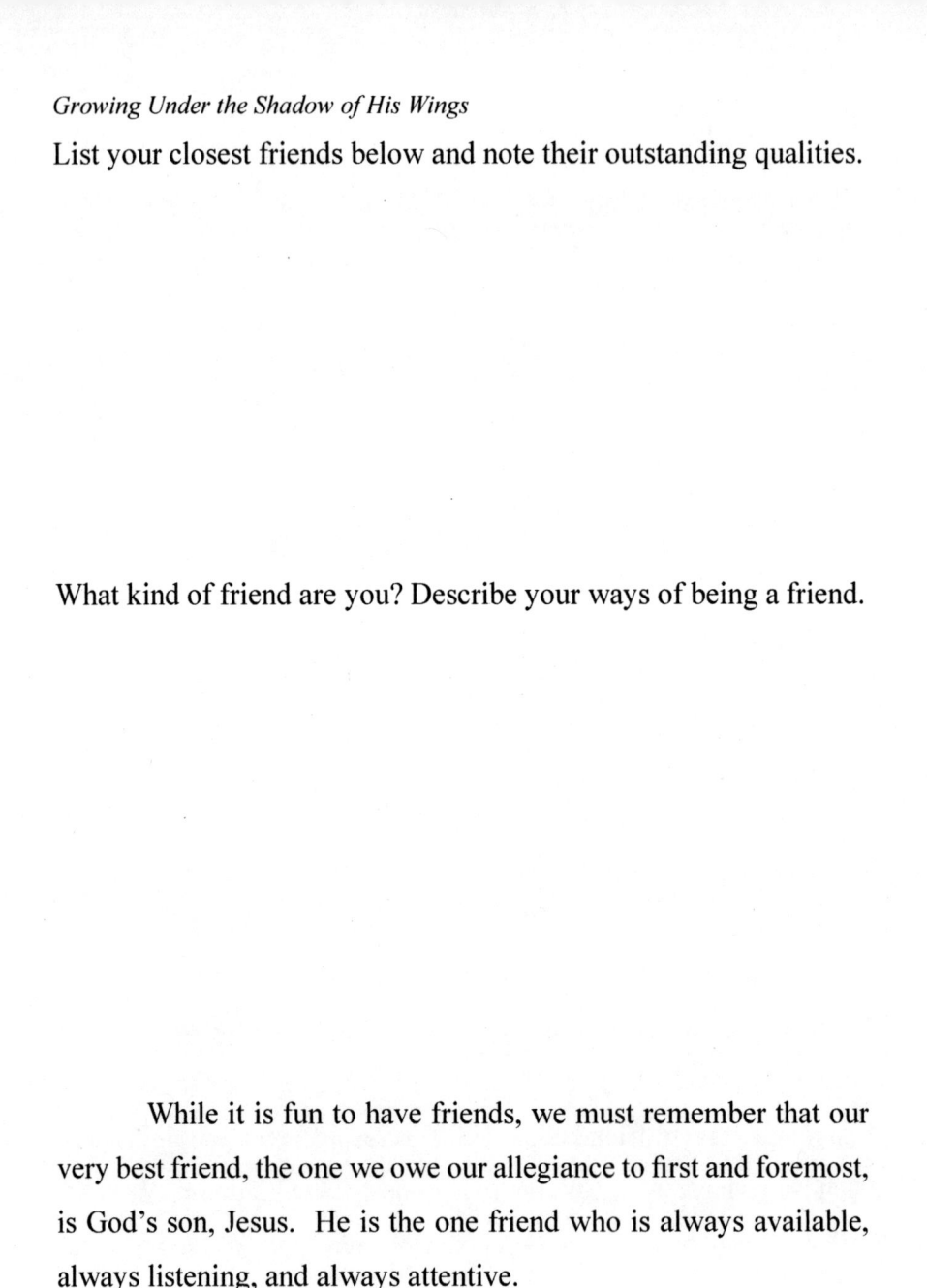

List your closest friends below and note their outstanding qualities.

What kind of friend are you? Describe your ways of being a friend.

While it is fun to have friends, we must remember that our very best friend, the one we owe our allegiance to first and foremost, is God's son, Jesus. He is the one friend who is always available, always listening, and always attentive.

"I love the Lord, because he has heard the
voice of my supplication, because he has
inclined his ear to me whenever I called upon him." Psalm 116:1

Friendship

How does it make you feel to know that Jesus, your very best friend, is always there for you?

In what ways can you be there for Him?

Growing Under the Shadow of His Wings

"The Lord knows our human thoughts;
how like a puff of wind they are." Psalm 94:11

Write a prayer to Jesus here. Tell Him why you can be His friend.

Friendship

Two Souls Knit Together

A beautiful story of loyal and devoted friendship is that of David and Jonathan in the First Book of Samuel. (1st Samuel 18:1)

Jonathan not only gives David his armor, sword, bow and belt; he saves his life. He accepted God's choice of David as king without jealousy or resentment, and he convinced his father Saul of David's worth.

We are all capable of loyal and devoted friendship. It requires over-looking one another's faults and recognizing one another's strengths and areas of quality. And it requires caring enough to rejoice in one another's joys without jealousy or resentment.

Can you think of a time when your friendship with someone was tested? How did you cope?

Would you change anything if you could live this episode over?

Chapter VI – Prayer Life / Methods of Prayer

> "Why are you so full of heaviness,
> O my soul? And why are you so
> disquieted within me?
> Put your trust in God;
> for I will yet give thanks to him,
> who is the help of my countenance,
> and my God." Psalms 43:5,6

To connect with God, we must engage in frequent and open prayer. We must communicate our thoughts no matter how inept we might feel. We can talk with family members, co-workers, friends, spouses, priests, or counselors, but there is no one who can provide the attentive listening of God.

Prayer is basically composed of praise and petition. To find peace for our soul, we must be willing to confide and trust, but appreciation and praise need to come first.

What can you praise God for?

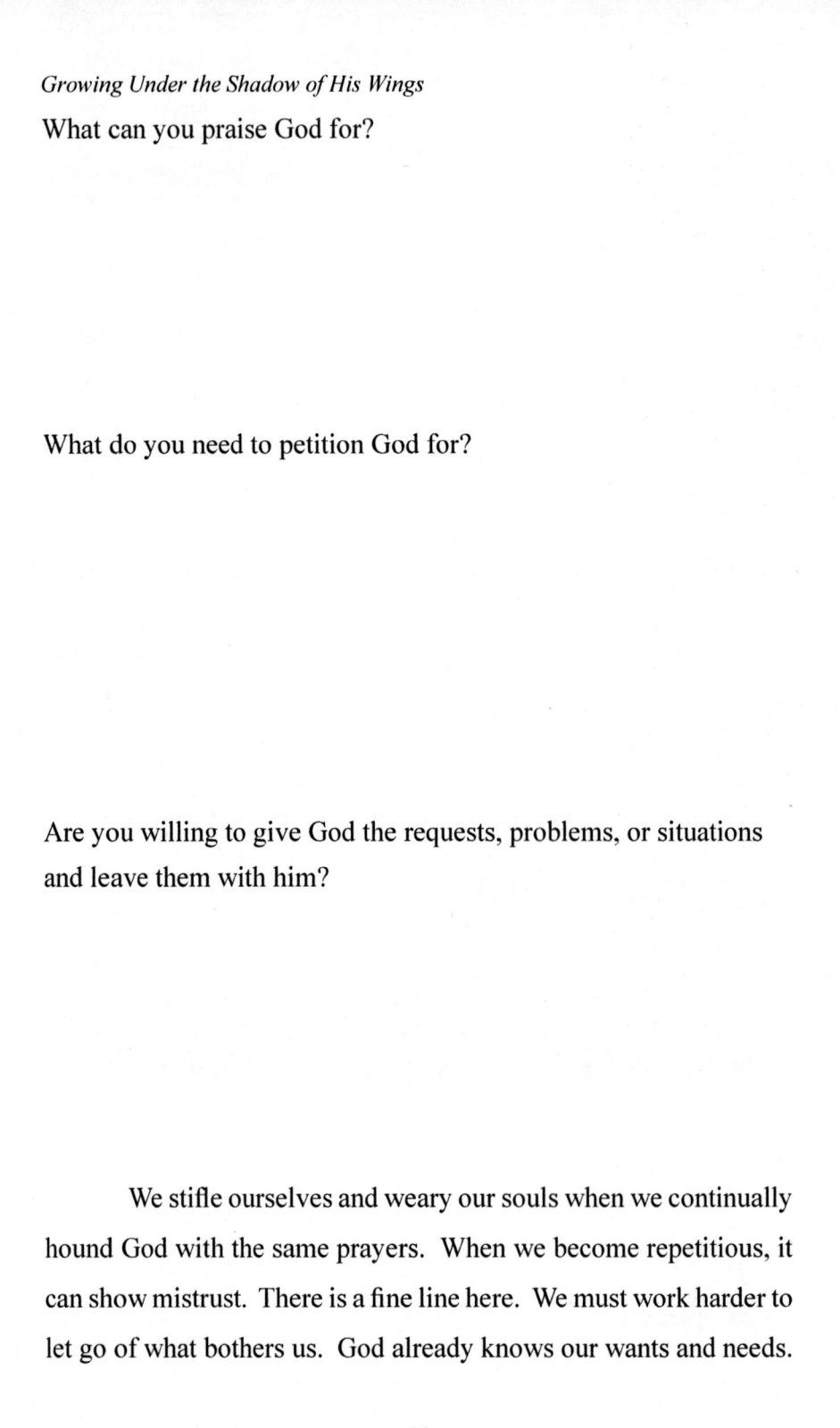

What do you need to petition God for?

Are you willing to give God the requests, problems, or situations and leave them with him?

We stifle ourselves and weary our souls when we continually hound God with the same prayers. When we become repetitious, it can show mistrust. There is a fine line here. We must work harder to let go of what bothers us. God already knows our wants and needs.

Prayer Life/Methods of Prayer

What request, problem, or situation do you take to God but continue to hold on to?

Write a prayer of praise for God – no petitions, only praise.

How do you feel not asking for anything?

Growing Under the Shadow of His Wings

Fill in the blanks for a conversation with God.

O God, I _____.

God, I need _____.

God, I want _____.

Dear God, do you think I could _____.

God, where is _____.

Please God, how can I _____.

God, you are so _____.

My God, with your presence I _____.

Read Psalm 4.

How does this psalm make you feel?

"Hear my prayer O God;
give ear to the words of my
mouth." -Psalm 54:2

    Hear my prayer, O God. Accept my humble and heartfelt praise and appreciation for all my blessings. Forgive all that is past and give me the wisdom to be receptive to your will for my life. Amen. (HPW)

Prayer Life/Methods of Prayer

<u>Prayer accomplishes three purposes;</u>
It brings us closer to God.
It helps others.
It helps us.

Prayer, while requiring self-discipline, changes our thinking. It causes us to become more desirous of a closer relationship with God and His Son, Jesus. Prayer keeps us grounded and praise keeps us humble.

I think it is difficult at times to pray and seemingly receive no answer. I have had to learn to be patient, to accept the fact that God's timetable is often far different from mine, and that he definitely knows best.

> "For God alone my soul in silence
> waits; from him comes my
> salvation." Psalm 62:1

Several years ago as I neared the end of a long and delightful teaching career, I felt somewhat disappointed that I had never been chosen Teacher of the Year for my school. There are thousands of teachers and only one per school can be chosen each year. But then a co-worker nominated me for a district-wide award, and I was chosen that year, not just for my school, but for the entire school district! I marveled at the wonder of it all and I begged God's forgiveness for my selfish desire, unbelief, and impatience. Then I gave him great and humble thanks.

We can be surprised and can find great peace when we accept God's timetable and seek his presence in prayer frequently throughout the day! Prayer for me has become an on-going "conversation" with God. I may be in heavy traffic, I may be walking for exercise, I may be sitting in a tub of bubbles; the beauty and comfort of prayer is the easy accessibility of our God.

Prayer keeps us grounded
and praise keeps us humble.

Methods of Prayer

Sometimes I hear someone lament, "I don't know how to pray." Or, "How can I be sure God is listening?"

I am convinced that God always listens, patiently and compassionately.

As to how to pray, there are many methods and styles of prayer. There are one-word prayers like "Help!" and simply "Jesus." There are quick prayers said in emergencies or desperation. And there are eloquently worded prayers composed with great thought.

God wants us to come to him and to come often. He wants our love, our praise, our respect, and he also wants our cares, our hurts, and our needs. I don't believe that God judges the punctuation or pronunciation of our prayers.

I pray as I leave my bed in the mornings. I pray as I drive in traffic. I pray in church, and I pray in the cemetery. I pray at work, and I pray during travel. I pray when I walk for exercise, and I pray while watching the evening news on TV. I pray as I close my eyes to go to sleep at night.

My prayers are usually short and sweet, like "Thank you for this day – help me to make the most of it. Amen." or "Give me the wisdom to be receptive to your will." or "Bless this dear soul who has entered your Heavenly kingdom this day." or "Thank you for food and air conditioning. Amen." Living in Texas all my life, I give frequent thanks for air conditioning! And I humbly pray for those who do not have it.

Growing Under the Shadow of His Wings

List your most frequent prayers here:

Do not let anyone tell you how or when you must pray.

Pray from your heart. When you can't think of what to say, just say the Lord's Prayer or the twenty-third Psalm.

Sometimes the best prayer of all is simply, "The Lord is my shepherd, I shall not want." Psalm 23:1

"But I will call upon God,
and the Lord will deliver me." Psalm 55:17

Some of my friends find the Jesus prayer to be a favorite:
"Lord Jesus Christ, have mercy on me."

The more we pray for others,
the more room there is for God to come in.
It is in prayer that we come closest to God.

Something to consider...

Lectio Devina

There are four steps to this method of prayer:
Lectio – listen to God's message through his word
Meditatio – reflect on God's word
Oratio – discuss God's word
Contemplatio – be silent and receive insight

Select a Bible passage of your choice. Read it carefully in the manner of Lectio Divina.
Record your thoughts here:

If you were to define prayer in only one word, what would it be? Conversation , plea, praise? Write your response here:

A favorite prayer is simply "The Lord is my shepherd, I shall not be in want."
It is in prayer that we come closest to God.

Chapter VII – Boundaries and Priorities / Choices

Boundaries and Priorities

> "The Lord looks down from
> heaven upon us all, to see if there
> is any who is wise, if there is
> one who seeks after God." Psalm 14:2

* We all have two portfolios – spiritual and physical.

Our spiritual portfolio embodies our belief system, our values, our relationships, our emotions, and our very souls.

Our physical portfolio encompasses our bodies and our health, as well as our material trappings – our homes, our classrooms, our offices, and our country clubs.

It is up to each of us to maintain and care for these portfolios.

Growing Under the Shadow of His Wings

      I can remember days when my engagement book was filled with activities – my sons' soccer games, Boy Scout meetings, piano lessons, my sorority meetings, Bible study, professional teacher organization meetings - and all this while I was teaching fulltime and being a single parent to two active young men. Whew! It wears me out just thinking back on those days. There were even mornings when I would arrive at my school with tears in my eyes from weary exhaustion. During this same time period, I was also trying to be supportive of my mother who was tending to the care of my ailing father. It finally dawned on me that I could not be a super mother, super teacher, super daughter, and super housekeeper all at the same time. I decided my sons, my job, and my parents were priorities – housekeeping was not.

List your priorities here:

Boundaries and Priorities/Choices

Now write a prayer about your priorities:

Do you feel pressure regarding any of your priorities and if so, why?

Occasionally, I will have someone telephone me and want to talk for an hour or more. I have learned to use my caller ID to screen calls, and I also have learned to be honest and explain that I can only talk for fifteen minutes and then I must honor other commitments. No one can infringe on our space unless we allow it. We are each responsible for our own boundaries. I need my private space and time. I need time to be with God, time to write, time to listen to music, time to watch the birds, time to take a nap, and time to relax in a bubble bath. I not only need this time, I insist on it, because I am a much nicer person to be around if I have had time and space to "fall back and regroup."

Growing Under the Shadow of His Wings

Do you ever go to an art museum or a park or even a cemetery alone just to soak up the quiet, the beauty, the peace that these places afford?

> "In God is my safety and my honor;
> God is my strong rock and
> my refuge." Psalm 62:8

What do you do or where do you go to preserve and refresh your soul's private space and time?

A Place of Peace
Helen Walters

I just want to go and be quiet
Where excuses are not made by me or someone else.

Where peace is not interrupted
And thoughts can roam free.

Where the love is real and pure
With no thought of gain or profit.

Where soft and warm, cool and quiet,
Clear and comfortable are safe.

Where feelings are safe no matter
Whether without or within.

Where prayer is ongoing,
Knowing I am listened to, cared for, forgiven.

Where joy is felt and treasured
And the soul needs no guard.

I just want to go and be quiet…

Growing Under the Shadow of His Wings

    The responsibility for maintaining our boundaries is crucial to our relationship with God. He should be our highest priority because without him, nothing else can be truly successful.

Rewrite your priorities here.

Have they changed any from your previous list?

Boundaries and Priorities/Choices

The most important ingredient in one's spiritual portfolio must be love – love for oneself, love for family, love for friends, but above all, love for God and an appreciation for His gifts to us.

In assessing the contents of my physical portfolio, I know that when it comes to health, good nutrition, skin care, multiple vitamins, and moderate exercise have to be priorities. Nothing in life matters if you don't have good health.

The key to simplifying both one's spiritual portfolio and one's physical portfolio can be found in the Bible. Philippians 4: verse 6 – 7 admonishes: "Be anxious for nothing, but in everything by prayer and supplication, with thanksgiving, let your request be made known to God; and the peace of God, which surpasses all understanding, will guard your heart and mind through Christ Jesus." (King James Version)

> "For God alone my soul in silence waits;
> Truly, my hope is in him." Psalm 62:6

Choices

Your best is your gift to God.

As we go through life, it is important to determine goals, set boundaries, and establish priorities. These all involve choices. In fact, almost everything we do involves a choice.

We choose to be kind or we choose to be rude. We choose steak or we choose chicken. We choose to marry or to stay single. We choose to walk with Jesus or we choose to walk alone. We all have done the latter, and invariably things go wrong when we think we can do it all ourselves.

Can you think of times when you chose to walk alone?

In thinking of choices, I cannot help but think of the gifts God has given us. He has given different gifts to each of us, but we are all of the one and same spirit. If you are called to be a computer person, be the best computer person you can be. If you are called to be a garbage collector, be the best garbage collector you can be. It does not matter if you are called to be a doctor or a fashion model, a lawyer or a priest – just make the choice to be the best for God that you can be.

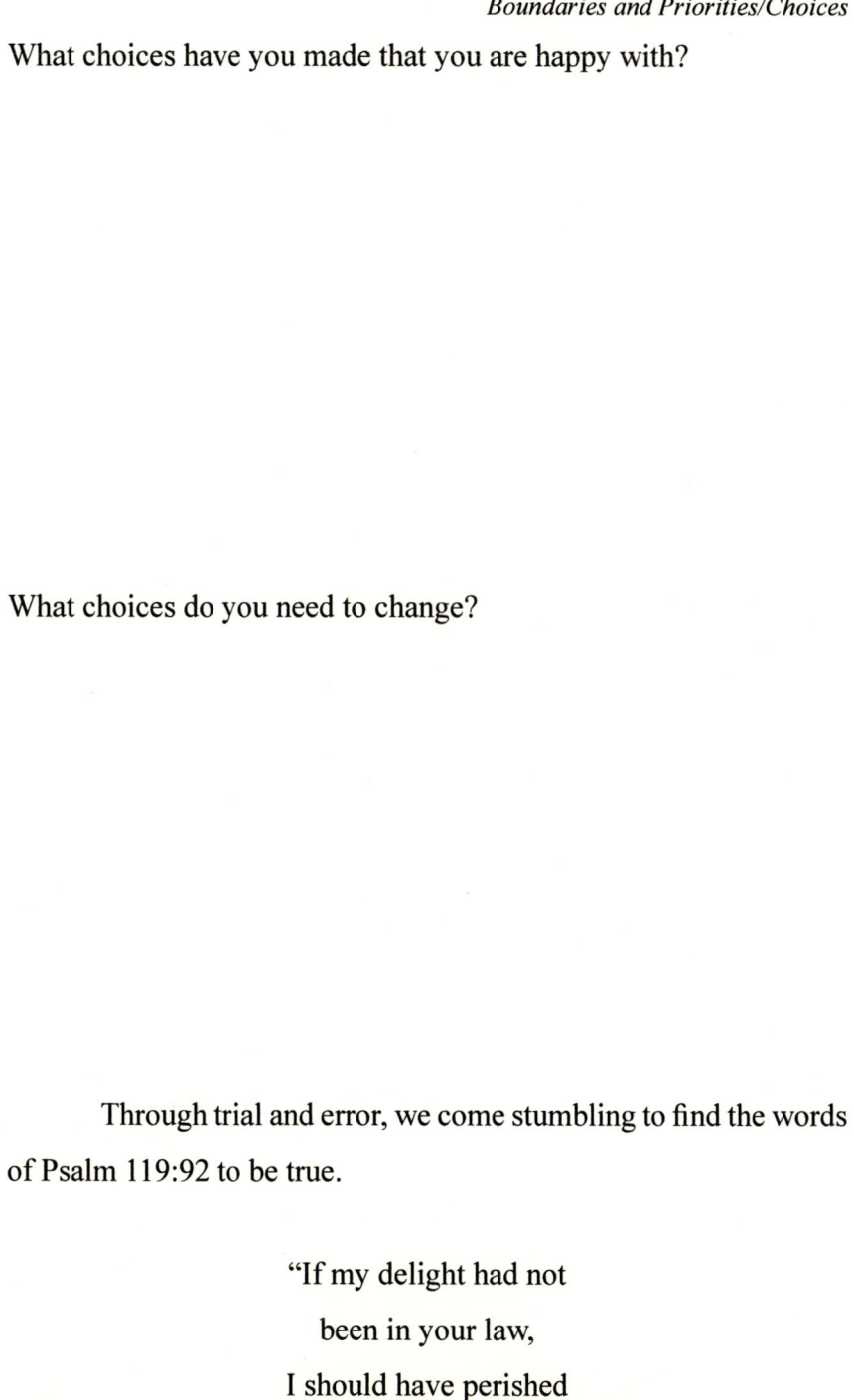

What choices have you made that you are happy with?

What choices do you need to change?

Through trial and error, we come stumbling to find the words of Psalm 119:92 to be true.

> "If my delight had not
> been in your law,
> I should have perished
> In my affliction." Psalm 119:92

Growing Under the Shadow of His Wings

Walking with Jesus is comforting yet empowering. We experience peace and confidence when we seek Him and when we trust Him.

The hardest thing for me is to have patience. Jesus does not rush about. He does not fret. He does not whine and moan. He radiates love and caring, kindness and compassion. And wherever we go, He is already there. We only have to choose to walk (not run!) with Him.

> "No good thing will the
> Lord withhold from those
> Who walk with integrity." Psalm 84:11

Simplify

When I travel, I don't like to waste time waiting in the baggage claim area. I'd rather be gazing at mountains or visiting with friends in a neat restaurant. It dawned on me several years ago that all you really need to pack is a toothbrush, a stick of deodorant, a few changes of clothes, and maybe a few stamps/addresses for postcards.

Keep things simple! It allows more time for joy.

* I first heard the idea of a spiritual portfolio in a sermon given by the Rev. Frederick Philputt. It caused me to pause and consider the fact that we all have portfolios other than financial ones.

Chapter VIII – Giving

"The Lord is full of compassion and
mercy, slow to anger and of
great kindness." Psalm 103:8

Our God is a great and loving God, bestowing many blessings on his undeserving children.

What or whom do you consider to be the greatest gifts you have received from our loving and generous God?

> "He has not dealt with us according
> to our sins, nor rewarded us
> according to our wickedness." Psalm 103:10

    I am humbled when I consider the gifts I have received from God. I am not worthy. I lose my temper on occasion. I am not the best housekeeper in the world. I sometimes forget to pray. But God does not cease in his goodness. In the Bible there is a verse regarding to whom much has been given, much will be required (Luke 12:48). We are called to give. Give first to God through prayer and worship; then give to others through kindness and caring.

Who or what can you give to in order to show your love for God?

> "How shall I repay the Lord
> for all the good things he
> has done for me?" Psalm 116:10

Detrimental Giving

The word "give" does not normally conjure up negative thoughts, but there are possible downsides. Have you ever known someone who spent an outrageous sum on a gift just to impress his or her peers? Or a father who gives all his free time to his golf buddies but none to his family? Or a mother who gives freely to PTA activities but is "too busy" when her own children come home from school? Or older persons, who, have left their wealth to the church but nothing to their struggling grandchildren?

There is nothing wrong with lavish gifts - a game of golf, being active in the PTA, supporting the church, and so on - but when the giving causes emotional and physical neglect or abuse, then the giving can become detrimental.

The following meet the criteria of detrimental giving:
1. When giving physically or emotionally devastates the giver
2. When care giving becomes all-consuming
3. When giving depletes the resources for everyday necessities
4. When giving is done solely for fame or recognition
5. When giving destroys the spirit of another

Can you think of instances of giving you have personally experienced that were detrimental?

The giver can also be harmed when the giving goes overboard and leaves the giver exhausted or penniless.

Can you think of any such examples?

    We want to always remember that our first and foremost gift should be prayer. Prayers to God of praise and appreciation and prayers for others to show our love for God and those he has created.

    Our soul flourishes when we give ourselves to God and others in holy prayer.

    Giving is a beautiful gesture if the giving comes from the heart.

    Giving should be more than simply writing out a check. Money is important. Money pays bills. Money buys clothes and food. Money sends our children to college. But money can lead us away from God.

    Psalm 15 defines who may dwell in the tabernacle of God. In verse 6 we read, "He does not give his money in hope of gain."

    If we give money, we should do so for the good of others, not for individual glory. We must work to spread God's kingdom.

    Sometimes we give money instead of time and talent.

Giving

Can you think of some instances when you could give someone your time (your one-on-one attention) or your talent (hammering nails, cooking, sewing, etc.) instead of just writing out a check:

Our soul flourishes when we give ourselves to God and others in holy prayer.

Chapter IX – Joy, Anger, and Grief

> "Lord, you have searched me out and known me; you know my sitting down and my rising up; you discern my thoughts from afar." Psalm 139:1

The same week that my elderly aunt died, I learned of two unborn babies, desperately loved and wanted, who died in their mothers' wombs. My aunt lived to age eighty-two, the last five years of her life in nursing homes, engaged in little more than sleeping. It is not my place to judge but it is hard to understand why some people live long years of seeming emptiness while others die young or don't even get a chance to be born.

A friend of mine just went through a very unpleasant divorce, his third. His new ex-wife cleaned out the house and their bank account. From all outward appearances, this man is kind, gentle, caring and generous. So why is he now divorced for the third time? Is his life a matter of making poor choices?

Growing Under the Shadow of His Wings

A young, beautiful woman studying to become a nurse is diagnosed with a rare disease for which there is no cure.

Many situations similar to these confront believers and non-believers alike. Anger rages if we give ourselves over to it.

What situations have you experienced that caused you anger or feelings of hopelessness?

"Bow down your ear, O Lord, and
answer me, for I am poor
and in misery." Psalm 86:1

"Lord, hear my prayer and let my cry
come before you, hide not your face
from me in the day of my trouble." Psalm 102:1

Joy, Anger, and Grief

Sometimes I think we must experience frustration, illness, tragedy, and loss in order to be aware of our need for God. We come to realize that he is our only source of reliability – the only one true and sure constant in our lives.

There is an opposite feeling, however. If we win the lottery or if our stock hits an all-time high, or the handsome guy or beautiful gal falls in love with us, then we are in immeasurable joy.

When have you felt the most joy?

I think my most joyous moments are those spent with Joel and Mark, my two sons. Things are not always harmonious and perfect every time we are together, but my two children are definitely the joy of my life. Giving birth to them, watching them grow, and now enjoying their friendship as young adult men has been and continues to be both a challenge and a privilege given me by God. I feel blessed.

One of my favorite prayers is the "Keep watch dear Lord" (P. 71) from the Evening Prayer service in the Book of Common Prayer.

Growing Under the Shadow of His Wings

It contains the phrase "shield the joyous." At first I could not figure out why joyous people need to be shielded, but then a nun explained to me that the joyous run the risk of turning away from God and becoming oblivious in their complacency and comfort.

We all need love and we all need prayers, whether in time of peace and joy or turmoil. We must never forget our soul's source of growth.

>Dear God
>When the happy moments come
>Help me to remember their source
>And give you thanks
>And when the sad moments come
>Help me to remember that
>You are still there
>To comfort and support me
>Still loving me
>Still wanting my love in return
>I am your child – forever.
>Amen
>-HPW

Joy, Anger, and Grief

"Great is the Lord and greatly
to be praised; there is no
end to his greatness." Psalm 145:3

Use this space to record any additional feelings of joy or anger you may have.

Do Not Lower Yourself

We all have the misfortune to encounter angry, frustrated drivers or rude and uncaring co-workers, not to mention sarcastic and cocky salespeople, etc. It takes strength, self-confidence, and compassion to not strike back, to not lash out verbally or haughtily. My wise and beautiful mother offered a most helpful statement many years ago. It has held me in good stead through many situations. She simply said, "Don't lower yourself to their level."

I might add it also helps to pray for any and all of the above. It really does make a difference! Try it the next time you are on the freeway!

"You, O Lord, are gracious and full of compassion,
slow to anger, and full of kindness and truth." Psalm 86:15

Joy, Anger, and Grief

"You have noted my lamentation;

put my tears into your bottle;

are they not recorded in your book?" Psalm 56:8

There is no neat package in which to contain grief. It comes in various ways and for various reasons. The most common and obvious form of grief is for the loss of another human being. But we can also grieve over the loss of a job, the end of a relationship or the lack of a relationship, the loss of a pet or the loss of self-esteem.

"The Lord is near to the brokenhearted

and will save those whose spirits are crushed." Psalm 34:18

List situations in your life that caused you grief:

> "I called upon the Lord in my
> distress and cried out to my God
> for help." Psalm 18:6

Who or what did you find helpful in your grieving?

> "The Lord upholds all those who fall; he lifts up those who
> are bowed down." Psalm 145:15

    Dealing with grief is very much an individual process. What works for one may not work for others. No one can tell another how to grieve. We can make suggestions and we can be supportive but we must realize that grieving takes time, patience, love and often, great effort.

Joy, Anger, and Grief

Think back to a time when you felt grievous. Fill in the blanks and record how you felt.

Oh God,
I feel so _____.
(hopeless, angry, weary, afraid, etc.)
Why did _____?
Was it _____ (my, his, her, their) fault?
How can I _____?
(go on, survive, begin again, forgive, forget, make amends)
Please help me _____.
Please give me the strength to _____

Usually the first reaction when grieving is denial and then we cry. Tears are a valid method of release as is chopping wood, planting flowers, going fishing, talking with friends, taking long walks, painting on a blank canvas and retiring for long naps. Perhaps not as valid or healthy is retreating from life. This is not to say that we cannot grieve alone but we must be careful to not become totally isolated. Grieving the loss of relatives and close friends is always difficult but I took the death of my beloved mother especially hard. Having to clean out her home and dispose of her possessions was wearying, emotionally and physically. I tried to work in her home only during bright, sunny daylight hours. I played beautiful, soothing yet uplifting music. I treated myself to special lunches and I gave great thought to which of her possessions I chose to keep.

Growing Under the Shadow of His Wings

And when the grief became overwhelming I would simply drive to the cemetery, sit on the grass near her marker and cry my heart out. I was not ashamed to call close friends and ask for comfort or companionship. And I prayed – a lot.

Losing a job, losing a companion through irreconcilable differences, going through a divorce, never dating or marrying, not receiving a promotion: there are many life experiences which cause grief. We can cope with any situation but only with God as our constant source of strength, nurturing and support.

> "You have showed me
> great troubles and
> adversities, but you
> will restore my life
> and bring me up again
> from the deep places of
> the earth." Psalm 71:20

And as hard as it may seem to fathom at the time, our loss or lack may be God's way of turning us in a different direction. Prayer is our key to survival and growth.

Reflect on incidents in your life when grief led to joy or progress:

Chapter X – Praise

"I will sing to the Lord, for
he has dealt with me richly;
I will praise the Name of the
Lord Most High." Psalm 13:6

How easy it is to go from day to day in a routine, turning to God only in a crisis. I sometimes shock myself when it dawns on me that I have gone through a day without talking to God. Prayer keeps me grounded and praise keeps me humble.

"My god, my rock in whom I
put my trust, my shield, the horn
of my salvation, and my refuge,
you are worthy of praise." Psalm 18:2

Growing Under the Shadow of His Wings

List here your reasons for praising God:

When complacency sets in, we do not think of praise. When a crisis occurs, we do not think of praise. Praise however, should be our first thought in prayer. Our God is so caring and compassionate, so deserving of our awe and appreciation, how can we not give him constant praise.

A challenging exercise is to <u>fast from petition</u>. To go on a fast has never appealed to me but I try from time to time to refrain from <u>asking</u> in prayer – to FAST FROM PETITION. It is hard to do. We implore guidance and healing, we beg forgiveness yet we often forget to give praise. Try praise and expressing appreciation to God only – no requests! Write your prayer here:

Praise

Read Psalms 135 and 136.

Do you think giving thanks is an adequate form of praise? Explain:

      I have always believed that no matter how terrible a situation, something good comes out of everything. If nothing else, we are drawn closer to God.

Can you think of such an example in your own life? How did you feel, and what happened? And did you find reason to praise?

Growing Under the Shadow of His Wings

Praise of God is appreciation. Praise of God is respect. Praise of God is reverence. Praise of God takes the focus off self and places it on our loving creator. When we acknowledge and revere the source of all love and caring we give our souls an open receptivity to the Holy Spirit.

O Holy One

I cherish your presence in my life.

I revere your Holy Ways.

I acknowledge your omnipotence.

Accept my humble, sincere praise of thee.

Forgive all that is past.

Keep me close to You and guide me on the path

Amen.

-HPW

Praise

"In God the Lord,

whose word I praise,

in God I trust

and will not be afraid,

for what can mortals do to me?" Psalm 56:10

How does praise lead to trust? Write your thoughts here:

Chapter XI – The Words of God

"My soul has longed for your salvation;
I have put my hope in your word." Psalm 119:81

If everyone is busy, there is nothing good on TV, and we are weary of worldly things, where can we go for sustenance? The Word of God! Turning to the Bible is never boring or mundane. It costs nothing but time, and it can't damage our health!

I have a friend who used to buy all types of inspirational books, seeking her answers from the wisdom of others. While there is sometimes great knowledge to be gained through this type of reading, she said she decided to read the Bible and nothing else. She finally felt comfortable and confident to make her own interpretations. And when she couldn't, she prayed for understanding and also consulted a priest.

Growing Under the Shadow of His Wings

> "Your word is a lantern to my feet
> and a light upon my path." Psalm 119:105

Read the above verse from Psalms several times. Say it aloud. Notice how a feeling of comfort envelops you. There is gentleness and strength, hope and guidance in this one verse.

> "My delight is in your statutes;
> I will not forget your word." Psalm 119:16

The Words of God

Below list some of <u>your</u> favorite Bible passages:

> "When many cares
> fill my mind,
> your consolations
> cheer my soul." – Psalm 94:19

This verse from Psalms is like a soft, warm blanket, soothing and reassuring.

When I feel like I've given my all and I'm weary with trying to be all things to all people, I find a psalm in which to rest.

To get quiet and rest in the word of God requires desire, discipline, and devotion.

> "For God alone my soul
> in silence waits." – Psalm 62:1

I love knowing God is always there to cheer my soul.

Be anxious for nothing.
Give humble and heartfelt thanks.
Give more.
Seek less.
Trust.
God is all we need.

Going to God

"I cry with my voice to the Lord,
with my voice I make supplication
to the Lord,
I pour out my complaint before him,
And tell him all my trouble.
When my spirit is faint,
Thou knowest my way!" –Psalm 142:1-3
(KJV&RSV)

Do not be wary of approaching God! He is all-powerful, omnipotent, awesome, and beyond our comprehension, but at the same time, he is also all-loving, all-caring, patient, compassionate, and tolerant.

This fact was again brought home to me quite vividly as I did a reading at a recent nine o'clock Sunday morning service. The reading was from the book of Genesis 18:20-33. Any parent or teacher would marvel (and maybe chuckle!) at the patience of our God as Abraham keeps hounding about God's possible wrath and the number of sinners to be avenged. We are so like children at times in our pleading, our whining, and our unbelief. God is indeed omnipotent, but he is also <u>very</u> patient!

See also the book of Luke 18:1-8 for a similar example.

Growing Under the Shadow of His Wings

> "I wait for the Lord;
> my soul waits for him;
> in his word is my hope." Psalm 130:4

Psalms of Reference

For the disappearance of fear: Psalm 27
For growing old with God: Psalm 71 & Psalm 143
For feelings of despair: Psalm 30
For penitence: Psalm 143
For joy from sorrow: Psalm 30
For trust and hope: Psalm 37 & 62
For serenity: Psalm 34 & 139
For calm: Psalm 11
For guidance: Psalm 119
For praise: Psalm 136 & 138
Record your favorites here:

Chapter XII – Sharing God With Others

> "I love the Lord, because he has
> heard the voice of my supplication,
> because he has inclined his ear to me
> whenever I called upon him." Psalm 116: 1

    This chapter is really about the word that strikes fear in the hearts of many – evangelism! The very word conjures up <u>what</u> in your mind:

Some people think of evangelism and they hear a street preacher screaming that the end is near. Others visualize trips to dark jungles or remote deserts. Others grab on to their checkbooks and hold on for dear life. Most of us do not have unlimited funds and private jets to make a "press release, token visit" to a very destitute and remote area.

Mother Teresa stressed that we only need to do a little bit at a time, right where we are.

Can you think of ways to show God's love and spread his word?

Sharing God with Others

We may not make the evening news or the cover of a magazine, but we will find favor with God. And that's what really matters.

Little things can be facial expressions, hugs, a casserole, a greeting card, a kind word, a yard mowed, a smile. If people notice you are at peace and usually content, they will wonder and eventually inquire as to how and why. This is when you really share God by letting them know that your love for God and his son Jesus, your faith, and your trust is what keeps you going. They will see that you are filled with the Holy Spirit. Your soul will flourish and they will want that, too.

The word evangelism is defined as a zealous effort to spread a cause. We can evangelize by simply being. Our behavior toward family, friends, neighbors, co-workers, and even strangers – can they see Christ in us?

List some ways you can share God where you are at this point in your life:

Growing Under the Shadow of His Wings

"In God is my safety and my honor;

God is my strong rock and my refuge.

Put your trust in him always, O people;

Pour out your hearts before him,

For God is our refuge." Psalm 62:8,9

Oh God!

*You know my path.

*You knowest my way.

Thou art with me

To the end of my days.

What comfort, what joy!

-HPW-

*After the King James Version and the Revised Standard Version.

The Favorite Psalm

The Lord is my shepherd;

I shall not be in want.

He makes me lie down in green pastures

And leads me beside still waters.

He revives my soul

And guides me along right

Pathways for his Name's sake.

Though I walk through the valley

Of the shadow of death,

I shall fear no evil;

For you are with me; your rod and your staff,

They comfort me.

You spread a table before me

In the presence of those who trouble me;

You have anointed my head

With oil,

And my cup is running over.

Surely your goodness and mercy

Shall follow me all the days of my life,

And I will dwell in the house

Of the Lord forever. Psalm 23:11-6

About The Author

Helen Price Walters, a resident of Dallas, Texas, has been a member of the Episcopal Church of the Incarnation since 1944. She is a lector and active in the Daughters of the King and the Community of the Holy Spirit Associates. She received Bachelor's and Master's Degrees from the University of North Texas and is a retired school teacher, having left the classroom in 2003 after thirty-six years of teaching. She is the mother of two adult sons, Joel Walters and Mark Walters.

Printed in the United States
22692LVS00006B/514-609